W9-DEL-086

Four Soar
and Roar

Pam Scheunemann

Consulting Editor, Diane Craig, M.A./Reading Specialist

ABDO
Publishing Company

Published by ABDO Publishing Company, 4940 Viking Drive, Edina, Minnesota 55435.

Printed in the United States.

Credits
Edited by: Pam Price
Curriculum Coordinator: Nancy Tuminelly
Cover and Interior Design and Production: Mighty Media
Photo Credits: BananaStock Ltd., Comstock, Digital Vision, Hemera, Image 100, PhotoDisc, Thinkstock

Library of Congress Cataloging-in-Publication Data

Scheunemann, Pam, 1955-
    Four soar and roar / Pam Scheunemann.
        p. cm. -- (Rhyme time)
    ISBN 1-59197-791-6 (hardcover)
    ISBN 1-59197-897-1 (paperback)
    1. English language--Rhyme--Juvenile literature. I. Title. II. Rhyme time (ABDO Publishing Company)

PE1517.S425 2004
808.1--dc22

                                                            2004049044

SandCastle™ books are created by a professional team of educators, reading specialists, and content developers around five essential components that include phonemic awareness, phonics, vocabulary, text comprehension, and fluency. All books are written, reviewed, and leveled for guided reading, early intervention reading, and Accelerated Reader® programs and designed for use in shared, guided, and independent reading and writing activities to support a balanced approach to literacy instruction.

Let Us Know

After reading the book, SandCastle would like you to tell us your stories about reading. What is your favorite page? Was there something hard that you needed help with? Share the ups and downs of learning to read. We want to hear from you! To get posted on the ABDO Publishing Company Web site, send us e-mail at:

sandcastle@abdopub.com

SandCastle Level: Transitional

Words that rhyme do not have to be spelled the same. These words rhyme with each other:

score

four

soar

more

oar

sore

pour

tore

roar

wore

Seth loves spaghetti.

He holds out his plate so Ava can give him **more**.

Jocelyn got a toy car for her birthday.

She is four.

The team is happy because they had the winning **score**.

Jack carries an **oar** over his shoulder.

Nan went to the doctor because she had a **sore** throat.

Claire's dad opened the umbrella when it started to pour.

Lillian and Dominic tore the
wrapping paper off of the
presents.

A tiger can make a very loud roar.

Evie always **wore** her pink hat.

Garrett and his dad watch their kite **soar**.

Four Soar and Roar

In a balloon, four friends did soar.

They were high above
the forest floor.

All of a sudden
it began to pour.

The balloon hit a tree
and the fabric tore.

hissssss!

hisssss!

Oh no!

17

They landed in a river,
near the shore.

18

They sure were glad
for the boots they wore!

They all loved the ride.
Bear said with a roar,
"Please can we soar
once more?"

21

Rhyming Riddle

What do you call a shop that sells paddles?

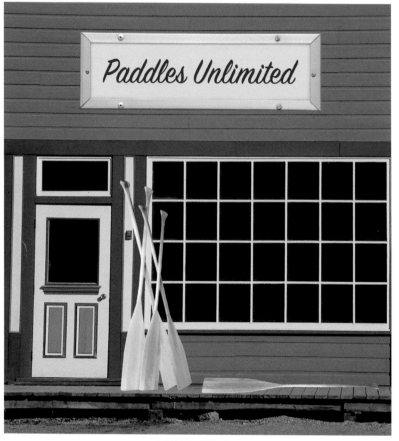

Oar store

Glossary

oar. a long pole with one wide, flat end that is used for rowing a boat

pour. to rain hard

shore. the land at the edge of an ocean or lake

soar. to fly high in the sky

sore. painful or injured

About SandCastle™

A professional team of educators, reading specialists, and content developers created the SandCastle™ series to support young readers as they develop reading skills and strategies and increase their general knowledge. The SandCastle™ series has four levels that correspond to early literacy development in young children. The levels are provided to help teachers and parents select the appropriate books for young readers.

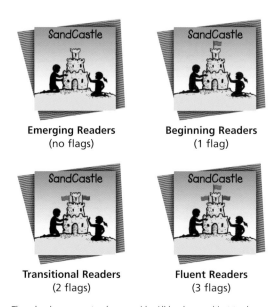

Emerging Readers
(no flags)

Beginning Readers
(1 flag)

Transitional Readers
(2 flags)

Fluent Readers
(3 flags)

These levels are meant only as a guide. All levels are subject to change.

ABDO
Publishing Company

To see a complete list of SandCastle™ books and other nonfiction titles from ABDO Publishing Company, visit www.abdopub.com or contact us at:
4940 Viking Drive, Edina, Minnesota 55435 • 1-800-800-1312 • fax: 1-952-831-1632